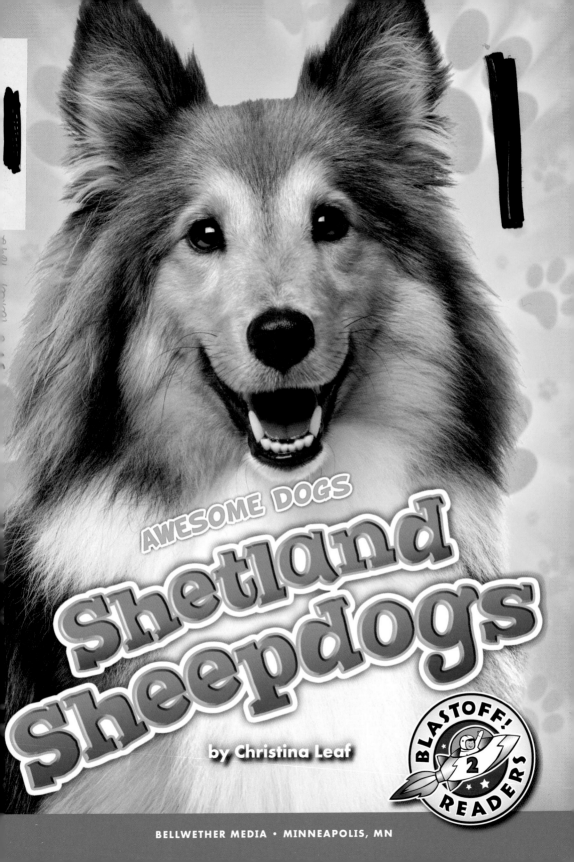

AWESOME DOGS

Shetland Sheepdogs

by Christina Leaf

BELLWETHER MEDIA • MINNEAPOLIS, MN

Note to Librarians, Teachers, and Parents:

Blastoff! Readers are carefully developed by literacy experts and combine standards-based content with developmentally appropriate text.

Level 1 provides the most support through repetition of high-frequency words, light text, predictable sentence patterns, and strong visual support.

Level 2 offers early readers a bit more challenge through varied simple sentences, increased text load, and less repetition of high-frequency words.

Level 3 advances early-fluent readers toward fluency through increased text and concept load, less reliance on visuals, longer sentences, and more literary language.

Level 4 builds reading stamina by providing more text per page, increased use of punctuation, greater variation in sentence patterns, and increasingly challenging vocabulary.

Level 5 encourages children to move from "learning to read" to "reading to learn" by providing even more text, varied writing styles, and less familiar topics.

Whichever book is right for your reader, Blastoff! Readers are the perfect books to build confidence and encourage a love of reading that will last a lifetime!

This edition first published in 2017 by Bellwether Media, Inc.

No part of this publication may be reproduced in whole or in part without written permission of the publisher. For information regarding permission, write to Bellwether Media, Inc., Attention: Permissions Department, 5357 Penn Avenue South, Minneapolis, MN 55419.

Library of Congress Cataloging-in-Publication Data

Names: Leaf, Christina, author.
Title: Shetland Sheepdogs / by Christina Leaf.
Description: Minneapolis, MN : Bellwether Media, Inc., 2017. | Series:
   Blastoff! Readers. Awesome Dogs | Includes bibliographical references and
   index. | Audience: Ages 5 to 8. | Audience: Grades K to 3.
Identifiers: LCCN 2016034478 (print) | LCCN 2016043000 (ebook) | ISBN
   9781626175594 (hardcover : alk. paper) | ISBN 9781681032801 (ebook)
Subjects: LCSH: Shetland sheepdog–Juvenile literature.
Classification: LCC SF429.S62 L43 2017 (print) | LCC SF429.S62 (ebook) | DDC
   636.737–dc23
LC record available at https://lccn.loc.gov/2016034478

Editor: Betsy Rathburn   Designer: Lois Stanfield

Printed in the United States of America, North Mankato, MN.

Table of Contents

What Are Shetland Sheepdogs?

Shetland sheepdogs are herding dogs that look like small collies. They are often called Shelties.

The **breed** is smart and full of energy.

5

Sheltie faces are friendly with long, rounded noses. Their ears stick up but fold at the tip.

Their oval eyes are usually dark.

Thick double **coats** cover Shelties. Their outer coats are long and rough. Beneath are shorter, furry **undercoats**.

Shetland Sheepdog Profile

ears that fold at the tip

fluffy ruff

long, thick coat

Life Span: 12 to 14 years

Trainability:

1 | 2 | 3 | 4 | 5 | 6

Hardest to train

Easiest to train

Fluffy **ruffs** surround the neck and chest.

Sable Sheltie coats can be golden to darker reddish brown. Blue **merle** or black coats may have tan markings.

Shetland Sheepdog Coats

sable   blue merle   black

All colors may have some white markings.

History of Shetland Sheepdogs

Shelties come from the Shetland Islands, Scotland. There, the dogs herded and protected sheep.

Scotland

N
W E
S

Shetland Islands →

Scotland

Visitors to the islands liked these small, friendly dogs. They brought Shelties to the rest of Europe.

The first Shetland sheepdog joined the **American Kennel Club** in 1911. His name was Lord Scott.

Today, Shelties are in the **Herding Group**.

People Pleasers

Shelties are **obedient** and like to please. They learn tricks quickly.

Some show off skills in **agility** events. Others learn to be **therapy dogs**.

Many Shelties are shy. They bark at strangers and when they feel uneasy.

But Shelties are loving and
protective with their families.

Pet Shelties still like to herd. They playfully round up their families.

Shelties love to keep their people in line!

Glossary

agility—a dog sport where dogs run through a series of obstacles

American Kennel Club—an organization that keeps track of dog breeds in the United States

breed—a type of dog

coats—the hair or fur covering some animals

Herding Group—a group of dog breeds that like to control the movement of other animals

merle—a pattern that is one solid color with patches and spots of another color

obedient—willing to follow directions

ruffs—areas of longer fur around the necks of some animals

sable—a coat coloring that is reddish with black tips

therapy dogs—dogs that comfort people who are sick, hurt, or have a disability

undercoats—layers of short, soft hair or fur that keep some dog breeds warm

To Learn More

AT THE LIBRARY
Gagne, Tammy. *Collies, Corgis, and Other Herding Dogs.* North Mankato, Minn.: Capstone Press, 2017.

Mattern, Joanne. *Shetland Sheepdogs.* Edina, Minn.: ABDO Pub., 2012.

Miles, Ellen. *Gizmo.* New York, N.Y.: Scholastic Inc., 2013.

ON THE WEB
Learning more about
Shetland sheepdogs is as
easy as 1, 2, 3.

1. Go to www.factsurfer.com.

2. Enter "Shetland sheepdogs " into the search box.

3. Click the "Surf" button and you will see a
   list of related web sites.

With factsurfer.com, finding more
information is just a click away.

Index

The images in this book are reproduced through the courtesy of: Eric Isselee, front cover, pp. 5, 11 (left);
Lenkadan, pp. 4-5; Tom Leaf, pp. 6, 9; Karen Walker, pp. 6-7; Verena Matthew, pp. 8-9; Juniors Bildarchiv
GmbH/ Alamy, pp. 10-11; cynoclub, p. 11 (center); Jagodka, p. 11 (right); Clement Morin, p. 13; otsphoto,
p. 14; Jne Valokuvaus, p. 15; Barbiturat, p. 16; AMusicorio, p. 17; OlgaOvcharenko, p. 18; Vagengeim,
pp. 18-19; Dmitry Kalinovsky, p. 20; Susan Chiang, p. 21.